FORTUNE

For John

fortunato ambo

Table of Contents

The Fortunes / 3

GUARDIAN BASTARDS

    Einstein's Brain / 7
    Edison's Elephant / 8
    Auden's Bed / 9
    Bishop's Pool / 10
    Dickinson's Walk / 11
    Tamar's Urn / 12
    Body of a Woman / 13

THE LUCK OF IT

    Hunger Artist / 17
    Open Season / 18
    Oracle / 19
    Melodrama / 21
    Theft / 23
    Tornado Weather / 24
    Earthquake Country / 25
    Smash / 27
    Weight / 29
    Judgement Day / 31
    How Orange, How Red / 32
    Tulips / 34
    Space / 35
    A Valediction: of the Booke / 36
    Jezebel / 38
    Open Book Surgery / 41
    Requiem / 42

KISMET

Friction / 47
Novel / 48
Second Sight / 50
Shut-eye / 52
The Siren's Promise / 53
Lilith / 54
Song / 55
Freak Love / 56
Homesick / 57
Move / 58
Genealogy of Heaven / 60
Peaceable Kingdom / 62
Property / 63
La méduse / 65
Arise and Walk / 66

ECCENTRIC ORBIT

Blacksmith Quartet
        The Village Smithy / 71
        St. Dunstan / 74
        The Farrier / 76
        Inheritance / 77
A Strip of Sky / 78
Odyssey / 80
Astrophel / 82

PROVIDENCE

Aliena Misericordia / 89
The Kindness of Strangers
        Moses / 90
        Swellfoot / 91
        Arthur / 92
Orphines / 93
Cuckoo / 94

Teacher / 95
Old Stories / 96
Home Children Poems
    Dr. Barnardo / 97
    Five Shillings / 98
    Flower of the Flock / 100
    Good Conduct / 102
    Bliss / 103

VIRTUE OF NECESSITY

Foster / 107
Brilliant Disguise / 108
The Family Way
    (i) Mother / 109
    (ii) Mother II / 111
Proof / 112
Unheimlich / 113
Rotten / 114
The Father / 116
Parenting Lessons / 118
Museum / 119
Human Genome Project / 120
Doppelgänger / 121
Prayer / 122
Farewell Symphony / 123

Notes / 124
Acknowledgements / 126

FORTUNE

The Fortunes

... the two benevolent planets Venus and Jupiter by reason of their kind and friendly nature.

—Joseph Moxon, *Mathematical Dictionary* (1679)

'twas I, I saw't

one planet with an eye, the hot aureole of a stone, the
burned stare of desert gathering clouds and lightning, no
rain. Jupiter means flying through air, then fog, then water,
then mud, then porous rock, an eagle breastplate, an oaken
staff, a sudden blow.

one planet closer to the sun, beauty in stone risen from
the foam, the jeweller's rock. Venus loves to laugh more than
she loves to love, steals wisdom from wit perched in a high
myrtle tree hung with sparrows and swans, but cannot stop
Vulcan from forging handmaidens of gold.

between them Earth swings, nudged by wide-shouldered
Sisters who hover in judgement before art, the death of stars
and the battle for a flag. Their lips are a stronghold against
hubris, their faces hang in the sky. Fate's shears, Fury's sting,
Valkyrie's choice.

the best laid plan favours the brave and hangs the hesitant,
shoves protests into a dark pit. Know up from down and
down from circumstance. The Fortunes serve what's hot, and
nothing else. Cross your fingers and swallow. Think small,
recall

rats live on no evil star

GUARDIAN BASTARDS

genius loci, filius nullius

Einstein's Brain

If Dr. Harvey mailed me a slice
of Einstein's brain, pulsing like a snare
drum, I would peel it from its slide and
slip it in my mouth, high
against my gums in the same hot
crevice where Alix hid his tiny jagged
blade that saved his life in Jakarta,
the serrated blade he carried
tucked against his cheek. He chewed
and swallowed as it rode his jaw,
a barnacle, a pilot fish. I saw its crescent
curled like a flatworm on his tongue before
he drew it like a tiny sword and balanced
it between his knuckles, a sixth

disjointed finger. The night crashed into
traffic behind our backs and Einstein's brain
floated in a dusty mason jar in an office
in Wichita. Dr. Harvey was a man of science,
and I am a woman with a mission, a passion for
the rest of the brain of the world's
smartest and saddest man. I would sew it
a green velvet pillow. I would play
Bach on the trombone, and take
care to take out the brain,
to brandish it only in
arguments about time, to consult it
about God's thoughts and relativity, Alix's
knife, Occam's razor. I would blow
that slim slide of cerebellum out of my cheek out
into darkness nestle it safe in the sleek
moulded cups of my second-best bra and do
the Charleston in bugle beads while I flirt with
disaster, nuclear or otherwise.

Edison's Elephant

Two men lead her on a rope that might
as well be a thread. She looks for the work
she expects to perform in harness, freight
to carry, flatcars to pull, the jewelled howdah
to bear a woman who waves to the crowd.
The elephant's forehead is a triangle of bone,
a slipped crown. She bows her head, allows
her bridle to be staked to the ground. Wires run
up her legs, her feet stagnant in a pool,
six inches of water, no more. The men leave
and she waits for hay or work, her toes cool
in the puddle until her feet begin to burn. She
peers through the smoke for the men who'll
rescue her from the fire in her legs. She can see
them bunched in a group; they do not move.
Then she buckles, a mountain plummeting in fog.

She falls on the rope; it breaks. She kicks out,
not like a beast of burden or might, but like a frog
under dissection, like an infant with colic at night,
like a dog tied behind a car and run to death. Now
Edison takes note of the exact voltage and current.
What was necessary to electrocute one elephant cow,
twelve years old, three calves. How she was meant
to bear weight, compliant. He discovers just how
to kill a willing giant, a great behemoth felled
as if shot, as though by thought repelled.

Auden's Bed

He shivered so cold at night in those
draughty mansions his hosts found him
one morning with a throw rug drawn
around his shoulders, a nubbly mantle,
a dusty caul. He'd unhook velvet
curtains and roll himself into their nap,
a learned sausage in pastry. Never
enough cover. His hosts once found
him asleep beneath a large oil painting,
legs and torso scrolled beneath an ornate
frame, his head atop it, playing
card turned soldier, a man flattened
by sleep and representation. Some chill
wind kept him restless. When he grew old
but no more warm, the spider in his bedroom
beckoned young men through a dozen
doorways, one by one, until they grew
close as skin. Bleak print,
the body swathed in quilts and paper,
an inky sarcophagus.

Bishop's Pool

Brazil's red clay is enough,
grass with blades tough as palm fronds,
conifers that surprise you with latitude,
the pool at the waterfall where frogs kick
across their small ocean, and crabs
raise pincers like Nova Scotia lobsters.

The green bamboo will age to a yellow
you will not live to see, cool
to the touch. You dare to grow
older under the mountain's humid
overhang, your toucan on the porch
in a big, small, smaller
cage, Tobias switching
his tail on off, on off,
then asleep. Oh. When

she gives you the studio, it is your place
to keep living, keep an eye peeled
for the vegetation's push from clay to air
like the statue she leaves you,
St. Benedict's ecstatic boy face,
lips rounded in awe,

like the first time you cut a fishing pole
with perfect flex, machete heavy in your hand,
frogs conversant at dawn,
the grass nothing like
Massachusetts.

Dickinson's Walk

After days when she sat by the high
window at the writing desk in her bed
-room in her father's house, eyes
shut to the gravel and grass
of her last walk, when the air
thinned and clouded
like bad water, there
were nights when

she thought she was made
of startled breath. She did not stand
like a sibyl on a fire
lit path burned through
the dry brush, a trail blooming
phosphorous spilling a dusty
glow onto her high

buttoned boots. She stumbled without end
through addled-curled sword grass, without
lantern or candle, knowing neither
distance nor destination, only that
she sought a standing
that was not
still.

Tamar's Urn

Go to, I pray thee, let me come in unto thee.
—Genesis 38:16

I was twice widowed
as you were twice sonned
when you banished me to a wraith
in my father's house. I returned
to your sight, a holy lady
by the crossroads, veiled,
unknown. Twice I asked
for your pledge, your ring,
your bracelets, a choice kid
from your flock, I asked for all
you would not give
your sons' wife, and you gave
to a whore as though you
were a pharaoh, as though
you did not count
each lentil in the pot. I am a truer
judge than you who would not feed
your sons' wife. Two boys stirred
within me at the hour of your leaving;
one will stretch his hand out,
thread his wrist through my womb
and withdraw, gracious as a king,
allow his brother to test the world
first for pain, then for privilege.
Twice sonned, I taste the Blessing.
I hold It in the urn of my body, I carry
a well's last sweet water that cannot burn.

Body of a Woman

She slumps as though her limbs were thrown,
legs askew, arms back, sweat and sleep in the folds
of skin. In Courbet's *Toilette of the Dead Woman*,
she sits propped in a chair, while two bent scolds
bathe and dry her limp feet. A mourning crowd
of twelve works in a dirge of slow thought
and cold comfort, airing linens for her shroud,
hearing her last day in Psalm 22 read aloud:
*my tongue cleaveth to my jaws; thou hast brought
me into the dust of death.* Her death a laying on,

their careworn hands. But renamed *Dressing the Bride*,
and sold later at auction, the same oil painting
shows her alive before her wedding, toil glorified.
In a brisk flurry, mothers lay the nuptial bed
with fresh linens. Two others smooth and spread
the tablecloth for the wedding feast. One girl reads
the Bible aloud: *he shall cleave unto his wife; and
they shall be one flesh.* Sisters wash and knead
the feet of the languid bride. (The corpse sleeps
one layer beneath; smirk and eyes painted on,

a careful hand.) Though she smiles, she keeps
her weary look, slouched on the chair like a sack
without grain. Eyes blank, lids with a sheep's
droop, back bowed, her long legs slack
as though she danced all night at the revel
in her honour, as though she drank her own
health many times. Now pinched with the devil's
headache, she's as limp as a length of rope, prone
to lie, an unfurled curtain, a ripped veil. Long
live the sleepy bride; the forger salvaged her

for cash in hand. He raised the female Lazarus
at her own wedding, where the guests will dance
and drink and disguise their daily envy in a fuss
about virginity. In principle, he was not wrong,
the old forger. He knew what was required.
Raise the bride, give her a smile but no tongue.
Cleave to her flesh, she's dead tired. Prop her
up, walk her down the aisle. Cue the choir.

THE LUCK OF IT

On Fortune's cap we are not the very button.
—*Hamlet*, II, ii, 232

Hunger Artist

All day we give chase, crash
through the brush, stumble on
our stick legs, fumble with clubs.
One deer belly a week's worth of hot
fat to cover our bones. The game
huge and swift, a doe lush with
oestrus. She makes the plain, open
grassland stretches her away.
She vanishes into the horizon,
printed round and dark on the sun.
She burns us until we splay
a green twig into a brush, twirl it
in a mix of ochre and spit
in the bowls of our blistered
palms, or spray mashed berries and
blood in a high arc from our pursed
mouths, paint a circle around her
sweet gristle.

Open Season

The hills red and orange above us. Deer
season opens today, bow and arrow
only for the first two weeks. She flexes
her biceps, she draws the bowstring
taut. The Blue Ridge highway whirs
beneath the truck, cab full of smoke and her
big talk, bed rattling with the spare and her half-
wolf hound, big as a pony and sporting
a single Cerberus head. Psoriasis
swarms him but he licks your hand, waggles
his peeling hindquarters. His rheumy eyes
stare as if he knew you when. Allergic to
grass and meat, skin scratched raw, his paws
pulse hot, an anthill above each claw.
He ought to be the worst hunting dog ever, but

he leaps to his feet when she whistles him up
and breaks for the trees, the *loup-garou*,
suffering glad hellhound. He lopes sideways
and looks over his shoulder, making room
in his pack for you. Riding back with the carcass
of the doe, shot clean and legal through the sweet
meat of her neck, he lays his head beside
her hooves and tries to sleep, dreams
a calamine bath for his fiery feet. Up front, she's
already making myth: *Little beggar stopped and
looked right at me, she wasn't afraid. Couldn't
ask for better.* The arrow in the doe's neck,
a compass pointing at cowardice.

Oracle

The boy who was born with his stomach
outside his body is no less than an oracle
          turned inside out
to read his own hieroglyphic organs,
intestinal rope rising like a cobra to
          the thin tune of his wail.
He breathes as though he was born to know
only the clear air of prognostication,
          the science of slip and say.
His tongue so swollen with good
omens, he cannot close his mouth, but
          he knows about high places.
Falling can be a plan, a leap. Chris says

she converted in kindergarten
when the nun who taught catechism
          caught her picking
her nose and made her stand in the hall. She
came back the next day with a note from
          her mother: *Our daughter
is no longer Catholic. Thank you.* She pulls
herself out of Dietrich's top hat, puts the pro
          test back into Protestant. She
wants to know who among us were baby
Marxists, hippy kids expelled or arrested. She
          smokes on the school steps,
I stick to columns of type with glue and

cheap ink. I know all there is to know about
the sting of my smartness. I lean on
        the dogma of physics
the way the unstoppable prairie drifts
against a snow fence. Galileo knew every object falls
        at the same rate, and I know
Galileo knows. The eventual truth
itches like a wool collar, knocks our knees, kicks
        ladders away from eaves.
        The cold is a poultice.

The oracle boy yanks up his shirt to show
the scar, the slash of skin and thread, a rip
        from stem to stern.

The truth is a parasite lying still as a tongue.

Melodrama

One summer I swam the air and watched
my own sadness with the same devotion I
spent on the sleek black hair tossed across
the bartender's forehead, the same way
I loved the humidity, the great equalizer,
every body at the bar spongy on their stools,
or sprawled like crustaceans on the patio. One
waiter flung thirty-five cents change to a customer
with a flip of the wrist, his eyes barely open.

All that June, ten waitresses competed for
the title, Most Tragic Girl, and by July,
I fell behind. All I had to my credit was
a bad break-up and my boring poverty,
one girl carried on a doomed affair beneath
her fiancé's nose. She wrote romance as
often as Shakespeare, was a slave to
a single revenge plot; cheat, confess, cheat
again. I was Chekhov's Sonya; I made lists with
my beautiful bitten hands. The Tragic Girl kept
her suitcases at my place all August; her
line of men paraded through, green as rushes.
By September, I was wan with the effort
tragedy takes. She left for the coast, and I
signed up for a hard chair and desk, hours
in the library—Strindberg, Ibsen, penance.

My phone spat out calls from her abandoned
men on the end of the line, gasping
at her absence. One called me
a liar, more than one wept, almost all were
drunk. I read of women who burned
manuscripts and shot pistols in their salons, who
taunted servants and coughed blood, women more
tragic but less mobile than she, women with better
plots who hadn't been swept away,
couldn't move on.

Theft

it was fun stealing
kisses you said you didn't
feel guilty after all
it's not theft this
stealing kisses from
another woman's man
because she was right
beside you because she was
beside herself she
watched you because
she offered generous
to a fault she didn't stop
you it was all right
stealing because you
kissed him as though you were
a child or an insect
crawling over a stamen
stealing pollen from
the flower it's how
nature works it's how
seeds spread everything
stems from that so you
sat on his lap
not that he was so great
looking it's just he was right
there so you crawled
over her to get to him
to kiss him look at
her kiss him

Tornado Weather

When she fills her lungs with close
air, humidity drowns her. The weak spot
on her lung, a flaw in a Persian carpet.
Her small son loves the garter snakes
in the woods behind the house, lets one
curl its narrow flesh around his wrist,
a living bracelet, but he won't hunt
without her. From the long grass, I keep
a close watch for the funnel that swallowed
her sister. Some poisons have no
antidote, this storm has no eye. The past
can say its own prayer. An ill wind blows

no good through her house. A poltergeist
tosses cups and chairs. A small brown harpy
turns a gasp into a breath and a sob into
a grasp, turns each day harder until
the heat breaks like an egg and a boy
falls asleep over his book of
salamanders and blue-tailed skinks.

A rain so cold that a dense mist
eats the trees, rusts the road signs,
softens the gravel beneath our feet.

She and I can dew our faces, wet
our hands, almost lose each other,
looming in and out, ghosts,
an arm's length away.

Earthquake Country

The earth moves during sex, they
say it carries a whiff of worms
and soil, until a tremor buzzes
the brimstone of six on the
Richter scale up your legs and
ages you like that. Rumble.
The window rattles like a motor
with a handful of coins flung
into it. The hair-on-cloth rustle
of twelve heads swinging up from
their books says it loud and clear—
twelve women will not fit
in the safe and narrow
space of the doorjamb. Roar.

The woman who has lived longest
in earthquake country shouts "Everyone
under the table!" and we slide from
our chairs to coil like lengths of rope
on the quivering tile and stare
through the forest of table legs. We are
eleven women, a diabetic and a lesbian,
a born-again Christian, a world
traveller, a party girl and her bookish
best friend, a Frenchwoman and a vegan,
a woman who saw falling
bricks crush the boy she lived with
in Mexico, and a prairie
girl so unknowing she thinks
earthquakes might be fun. We hold on
to nothing, lemurs shaken
from branches. Waiting out aftershocks.
The bravest tells a joke so dirty
it shocks the bloom of panic

from the eyes of the one girl
no one knew. The only
mother among us bolted
out the door before anyone else
moved. In the city to the south, the world's
richest man sits on a stage and hundreds
shriek and scatter. Across town, a red
ape called Peter swings in a shuddering
arc in his cage, his sad simian eyes
say *human see, human do,*
this much and more he always
already knew.

Smash

Slow, this moment before metal on
metal. I close my eyes
                    let the dark
carry the crash, a sharp
crack like gunpowder lit
in the sudden small room of the car.
Air raw as fibreglass. The seatbelt
punches my sternum—the sternest
bone, the wooden hanger
in the body's walking closet,
the unbending teacher who keeps
the student body in line.

    A body at rest
tends to remain at rest, a body
in motion tends to remain   *in motion;*
if a body is at rest inside a body
      in motion, a rested body
arrested in flight by a moving body

    we call it

        an accident
        a miracle

        (saved by
        St. Christopher
        and the dash
        board Virgin
        his broad back
        her blue view

    we see it

Smack of car against car.
A clenched fist, an open
hand. A hanger yanked
askew. The bruise a crushed
dahlia beneath my skin. I take it
to the bridge above the river,
watch the ice break open. A
homemade hockey rink drifts
beneath, its blue lines blurred by
thaw; it teeters on the edge
of the dam, then tips,
slow, slow, slips from its cold
fulcrum to smash

                            this is my
                            flesh at
                            rest, broken
                            open for
                            view

Weight

The boom and crush of metal. Your body falls for a month.
You wake at eight to fall asleep at noon, acrid tang at the
back of your tongue, bad oranges. You camp out in the
waiting room and struggle to your feet when the nurse
mispronounces your name yet again. List your symptoms
once more, every time. You remember your medication, the
chemical and brand name. Impress your doctor. Spend your
waking hours devising similes for the pain that squats in
your shoulder and rattles up and down your arm.

*Like a yoke across my shoulders, like carrying milk pails, like
anthracite, like a hump. Like hail on a windshield, like a
poured concrete sweater, like rusty armour.*

You turn into the Golem with its body of mud; you stalk the
edges of the *shtetl* to protect it from evil. No more accidents.
Your doctor looks up from under her orange hair and shifts
in her little bird bones. You could take her three out of three
falls in the wrestling ring, break her across your knee like a
broom, snap, even with your bad arm, she'd sear like a log in
fire, sizzling with what little fat she has.

She drops her voice to a whisper when she recommends massage therapy and writes out a list of exercises, misspelling shoulder. You say nothing. The mud hardens over your mouth. Your massage therapist is named Attila and he doesn't ask how you feel; he says nothing when he sees your scar like a lightning bolt, your vertebrae a string of flawed stars. He lifts your arm, your breath flies from you

red dogs, grey hair, plate, stone, air.

Judgement Day

In the chill of March, a troll with a
trumpet blows scales and gospel beneath
the wooden bridge across the road,
in night air so cold you would swear
his lips will rip at the touch of metal. In
half-gloves, he tips the three valves into
a brace of notes, and his frosty breath
urges the tune upwards, a whale nudging
its calf up to a first breath. Reveille.

The brass vaults the stiff air until
you freeze in place, think the horn
must shatter from the effort of pushing
glissandi into the cracks of night.

The pitch enters your lungs, a clutch of
high notes you store away until
the thaw, when the ice melts on
a long curve of road and marches
you away—with troll and bridge—
straight into the singing mountain.

How Orange, How Red

The grey day splits open, a sodden
box, bottom burst with the weight of
rain turning to snow. Flurries,
dirty tufts of uncarded wool,
a boil of locusts come too early
to strip the green. Wasps released
from their perfect porcelain hive,
bent on revenge. If you look too long,
the snow will fool you into
falling upwards.

Hatched by central heating, a ladybug
crawls up your bookcase, reads
the Braille of spines. Knows it is a sin to kill
the six-legged. She flies
to your knee, obedient
as a spaniel. Her wiles save her,
flirty unexpected wings, glossy
back that shimmies like a go-go dancer.

Each summer, the girl next door counts
ladybugs in her yard, noting
how orange, how red, what number,
what size of spots in a tiny spiral
notebook.

When the swarm of snow melts,
you buy a branch studded
with inert orange pips,
a delegation of ladybugs on the
candelabra of twigs. They wait
for the sun to warm them
to flight. If you plant
the branch in the earth beside
a rose bush, the ladybugs will
flit, bright helicopters above
a landing patch of thorns.
They will perch on your shoulder,
shout so no one else can hear your house
is on fire your children
are gone.

Tulips

In May, boys with pastel heads
lean down the alley, slouch in
ripped t-shirts and high-tops on
the third-floor fire escape, kibitz
beneath cadmium yellow hair. Amethyst
blotches the pale skin of another's nape
where he can't see the blueberry stain,
the mottled mark of Cain sugaring his neck.
Still another boy chases a Frisbee in the park,
loses his green head among leaves.

Fugitives from a crayon box, they skitter down
to drink by the river, low this year,
rocks bald above the current.
Stripped of ennui by their glowing heads,
each trip for cigarettes is epic,
each beer a sock in the eye. Battery
acid charges their brains, brilliant
blooms, jewelled Easter eggs,
dye seeping into their cauliflower
lobes blown hollow.

Space

She quits her job measuring space
the same fall that the sun traps her,
a chameleon caught lettering itself
onto the pages of a book. Portents
are mixed. She drives with one eye
shut for fear the deer by the roadside
will throw themselves beneath
the wheels of her car. Rabbits she knows
sprawl on the lawn like Cleopatra,
lounge on a grassy barge, hind legs flung
behind them like an extra pair of ears,
a scarf, a soul tugging at the body.

She leaves space like a husband, a lake
in September, a ball at midnight. The sky
crowds the earth. Praises for Apollo split
the air. But she remembers Cassandra and pushes
no more rockets off the tips of her fingers, no
more capsules splash and explode. Laika
circles the earth, a slack lump of fur. She
leaves her instruments measuring danger
to the body, and shops Atlantic
City for soccer socks and a green plastic
triceratops for her son, who has reached
the age of reason. Three thousand men polish
their glasses in a hall,
wait to speak.

A Valediction: of the Booke

January teaches the sun
an unruly chill; I must read
forty books before April.
My poetry professor swore
an oath against love last fall,
but now has been dropped
into it like a rock in oil.

My professor sports a chunky
gold ring and a mouthful
of peaceful teeth, takes more breaks,
tells more jokes. The smart girl
in my Donne seminar unwinds
her thick rope of hair, a sensual
shock that falls to her waist, pools
like syrup across the long table.
On dark library afternoons, she
studies with her lover, his spill
of hair as long as hers, two dark
heads rapt with text and each other,
Siamese twins joined at the temple.
Solitude is for other people.

The professor wears a new silk
shirt and a watch that runs slow as sugar.
We argue about Donne's metaphysical
conceits, his ordered crush of language,
disparate feet of a compass stilled,
pointing to love and grief.

The professor scribbles
A's on a tall sheaf
of unread papers, fiddles
with a pencil and watches icicles
on the eaves lengthen to spears.
A long brown hair frills
across my desk. I wind it
around my pen ten times until
it breaks. Ten more weeks
of winter. Ten weeks until
the feet of my compass will reach
far enough to draw an arc,
before icicles melt to fill
every available vessel,
even the cup I carry to class,
a curve of liquid nudging
the rim, easy to spill.

Jezebel

Behind the frosted glass
door of my office, I write

              a woman   her word

become flesh, oiled, holy
with ink and dust.

I write
        the bodies of men
        naked, not nude.

I write
     penis
     seven times on a page—
the Jesuit in the office
               next door shifts
and shuffles.   He and I,
     zealots for knowledge,
but   when he reads me,

his collar tightens,
      his hands flap and fall

sparrows before the eye of providence,
      the evidence before his eyes.

I write *breast*
        tongue
            transubstantiation

and Sister Justine knows I'm Protestant
every morning   my pestilence
            scuffs by her door in
            cowboy boots, piping
Good morning Sister!
                and she narrows her
                            eyes, petulant.

Maybe she's heard
            about me   and the penises.
Maybe she fears the world will be
                hard on
                    women like me.
Maybe she's yet to turn
                the other cheek
about the way the chapel window
exploded when I walked by,

            the Pieta in pieces,
all that coloured glass peppering
the sidewalk.   Sister Justine had
to sweep up.

        I write
            neck
                mouth

I am careful and busy and
            they take my pen away.
I stand in the hall and
write in the dust with my toe   *beloved*   *beloved*

when they arrive   a murder of crows,
I show them   the clean unlined palms of my hands,
and they lift me onto their shoulders as if
                                        it's a parade,
as if I've scored a goal in overtime,
and I sing
                    oh ye
                                daughters of Jerusalem
                    oh
        oh
            oh

and then I'm out
        in a snowbank

    with the heat of my breath, I write

            how beautiful   *thy feet in shoes*

Open Book Surgery

Curl your fingers beneath the ribs.
With a steady grip, pry apart. It will
split less easily than a walnut. Yank
if necessary, until it divides into
two limp flaps flanking
a pulsing hollow.

Keep your gloves on.
Peel away the layers of tissue, sheet by
glutinous sheet. They will ease back with
little trouble if you are firm
enough. Reach

                            deep into the cavern.
Your hand will disappear
up to the elbow.
You may think
you are cleaning
chickens and if you are lucky
or skilful,
or both,
you may draw out the pith,
pulsing with letters &
ampersands.
Be forewarned.
Ink will stream down your arm,
a surface vein of pitch.
Staunch with a blotter
and place it in a sterile chamber.
Refrigerate for transplant.
Note all sources.

Publish findings.

Requiem

Cold spring night in the city of rivers
and bluffs, she and I walk
downtown, pass a hand-lettered
sign in the window of the Varsity
Liquor Store: *Closing Sale—20% Off*
Hard Liquor Only. We pass
the warming powers of discount
rum and a man dances a jig
in the parking lot, shouting *Yes! Yes!*
at the sight of us, two ecstatic votes for
our dark blazers, our bright hair, our chunky
shoes like small trucks shifting us forward
into sartorial ruin. *You're*
lawyers, I know it! he cheers—
counsel at last. We hate to tell him
no. Tonight we trade in
our good grammar, scurry
past the open door of a bar where

a happy fight howls, but
the sound of chairs splintering
can't cover the moan of a woman
crouched against the wall outside;
whose death hiccups her speech,
what hinge of history? We find an Irish pub
and blarney the bartender into making us
margaritas, an icy red blur. The Rocket
died today; trophy heads of old players
sprout from the big screen, red-eyed bison
bearing the musty humps of hockey hierarchy.
A short man in voyageur buckskin smells of
bear. He chats up every woman in
the bar, smoothes his mullet, asks about
making love. In a canoe. He eyes us

and paddles on because we are too
tall. We might be the law, voyeurs to the fur
trade. A man with a guitar and
a thousand voices sings "The Log Driver's
Waltz"; we down our drinks in one and slide,
replete, onto the dance floor, good
Canadians, good girls at forty, good
God, we are pleased completely.

KISMET

. . . whether love lead fortune, or else fortune love.
—Hamlet, III, ii, 209

Friction

The second official day of spring.
Snowing. The mail brings an account
of someone else's affair with destiny.
She scribbles alchemy; her lover,
mercurial, voluble, spills
into the ink beneath my hands.
She defies the cold, her words
dew my throat

like night grass, like jonquils
beneath a rain spout, like a burst
melon, like the first time you put
your hands on my head and drew
my hair straight back over
my skull, slick as a seal.

Letters about love, anyone's love,
rub against me like cats, claiming me,
laying their musk, oiling
their muscles. However
I wish, I cannot keep the world
away; it bumps against
me on a crowded bus, thrusts
packages into my ribs. If it was just
me, I would not balance
you against fate—one side
does not always equal

the other. But when the moon washes
my room with milk, I know
the long bones of your hands glow
above the deep creases at your
wrists, bracelets of fortune.

Novel

Boy meets girl in Winnipeg, and who cares?
                        Hugh MacLennan reporting on the American view of the
                        Canadian novel in 1957

Who cares other than the boy, the girl,
their families in their Winnipeg houses
drinking Winnipeg coffee and remarking on
the famously dry cold. Who cares if
her neighbours lie awake in their uneasy
beds to hear his car pull
up late at night. It is enough to know.
Their single friends drink at the Toad
or the King's Head. Their married friends
invite the new couple over for a barbeque
and cribbage on Saturday.
The grocer rings up her purchase of
an extra litre of milk on Sunday mornings.
The mechanic tunes his car to purr
the neighbours to sleep. The churchwomen
at the rummage sale give them a good
price on a goosenecked lamp. Their mutual
friend claims she made the match. (So do
their bosses, colleagues, teachers, blunt
mentors and blissful brothers, so does the waiter
with the too-long moustache who saves a
booth for them and tells them how he invests
his tips in the stock market. So does the woman
who never laughs at the French they speak
in her St. Boniface dry cleaners.) Boy meets girl
in Winnipeg, in Saskatoon, in Medicine Hat,
in Lethbridge, boy meets girl in corduroy
or denim or goalie pads, girl meets boy

in anticipation, in silence, in hope, in the
knowledge that it's not literature, it's a story
only she or he can tell. Declare Canada a
banality-free zone, and write of loftier
lives, finer tones of skin and lethargy lit by
the Parisian sun, that quality of light.
Hugh cares.

Second Sight

Your father bought the house where
you were born because he saw the Russian
olive in the front yard. Nodded at
the greengrey leaves, knew the tree
would please her, your mother big with you.
The olive tree kept its leaves the winter you
were born, spoke to her when no other
leaves hung in the cracking cold.

It is almost summer when you see
a Russian olive shading the four
empty rooms I chose for their mix of light
and shadow. Long after midnight, you steal
up six flights of stairs, and put your finger
to your lips before you draw open the door.
A green metal wheel spins straw into
gold in the dark. The green wheel
spools the elevator cable, lifts and lowers
the cage, that box of gravity
and trust. The cable a slim thread spun
in the crux of giant scissors, the green fly
-wheel stolen from Charon's
ferry. We look for a reason to scare ourselves,
and find it. Once we've seen the cable
draw bodies up like water from a deep
well, we cannot quite shut the door.

Sunday visits with your father
stretch by seconds, then minutes.
Equinox approaches, lengthens days,
reckonings. The Russian olive speaks
at my window, its leaves recall the old
gift, second sight, a chance to see
what we have turned from, whom we have
turned to. The future pooled, loose
shoelaces around our feet.

Shut-eye

Up too early and rained out of work,
fall back to sleep, hard enough
to retrieve the lost hours from where
they thud to the ground on the far side
of the reservoir. The gift of shut-eye.

Dead to the world, sprawl off the edge
of the mattress, let the door swell with
humidity and age. Rain sweeps
the road, a falling wave. All day
the man upstairs walks barefoot on your
ceiling. He maps out a route from room
to window to door, reads the walls.
The elms stand as straight as rain,
lights flicker, thunder or a small seizure.
Fat drops stipple the reservoir.
The rain hauls the sky through a sieve,
pools onto the street where you first
stood, looking up at the dark glass,
wooed up to these rooms, convinced to
stay for a little while.

The Siren's Promise

No matter where you sail,
I will find you by echolocation,
sound waves against still bodies.
I will swim the ocean of your bed,
my eyes rimmed red with salt.
I'm that kind of girl. Song curls
like a conch behind my lips,
but for you, I will sheathe my
perfect pitch. The only map
to you is so old I must read it with
my hands, follow the watermarks.
No sextant can pinpoint
my longitude and latitude. I float
not three yards off your bow,
no message in a bottle, but
patient as a cork. Untie yourself
from the mast. I will lie
upon your tongue, a vestigial tooth,
a chambered nautilus. I am the ocean
borne forward on two white legs, I fill
your room with the scent
of seaweed and mollusc.

love the conversation inserted into the poetic

Lilith

Sleep covers you like a sheet, a dense
web of skin that sloughs lines
from the corners of your eyes, sets
your jaw stern as a centurion. I know
the honeymoon's over, but hard work
suits me. Better than bliss. I roll up
the sleeves of my pyjamas and wait
for the bed to give beneath the weight
of her ghost between us, and there she is.
She flits across our skin, swamp
fog, or one of those tongues of flame
sailors will spot from the crow's nest,
and then fear for their wits. I am not
cowed. I will bury her at sea, wrap her in
stiff canvas and tilt her plank, listen for a
grey splash, her dive into
the ocean's bed, I'll tug up to her chin
her blanket of salt and silt. Do you
know me yet, brimming with brio and
foam? I am everyone's fool. I will
dig her a grave at the crossroads. I will salt
the ground with my own blood. I will gather
sticks for her pyre and guard you from
the lick of flames. What's to fear. We are
left with a caved-in sky and the clothes
on our backs, and no
longer believe the face carved into
the moon will deliver us from
evil, or from love.

Song

You ask me to sing
around the house, ask
as though snatches of song
would tune the days when we
fell together with a clang,
a hammer flung, a bang,
pliers whose twist
reduces everything to dust
and harangue. It's been years since
you swung through the door and boom
eranged your way back.
I read you the way I would
read my own
palm or the entrails
of a goat whose throat rang
beneath my blade.
I know you as I stir
that slick tangle of flesh
with a stick and feel a twang
quiver up the rod, a plucked

string   an open note. I sing.

Freak Love

Bless the way
one shoulder blade juts
from your back,
a shark's fin, a shovel
of bone. Bless
the muscles that keep it
hanging, a weapon
on the wall of your back.
There. Bless
the tendons you were born
without. Bless
the stone each woman and
man of the ten lost tribes
took upon their shoulders.
It is the crown of Job.
Rub it for luck. Bless
the torque in its scaffold. It is
a handhold on the steep cliff
of your rubber body, a rudder
in the wind, redder than
repair, the hinged door on
a control panel swung open
for inspection. Tug the rope of
your spine into place, and
your skeleton shifts
one sixteenth of an inch
to the left in its red
union suit, its issue of
blood and tissue. Bless the
unknown in this unbalanced
equation, bless the rogue
chromosome.

Homesick

The deer eats leaves off the plum,
skirts the arbutus, scrambles up
the slope when he's had his fill.
A yearling, buds of antlers no longer
than my hand, used to easy food
this second spring. He will
not spook. By the spruce, he shoots me
a glance to show
                            leaving was his
idea. You drank the holy water from
the bottle on your father's dresser, sure
at first that it would make you better,
smarter, bigger, then later, sure you had
invented a sin for which there was no
absolution. Indulgence tastes like plum,
sin like water, the shadow of memory
                            a cat that slips
the corner of a couch, a glimpse of dark
in day, some animal whose
curiosity we are craven
enough to call love the brief
hallucination we call homesickness,
we call home.

Move

We drive west for three days and do not call
home. Stiff-backed, we ignore the flat slow pull,

muscles straining to double back or go,
throats hoarse with the week's pack and haul.

A man with a black patch over one eye slows
at the sight of us on the road, his bleary pupil

watching for signs of passage or expertise, how
we follow this tattered map, how we read the signal.

Greeted by the dog without eyes who lifts his nose,
a guard to sniff for food or danger in the hall,

we unpack our worldly goods, everything we own
tucked into a bag and rolled into a newspaper ball.

We have woven a path between towers of crates, a tableau
of kitchen chairs, boxes of books, a Formica table,

the old green couch, six suitcases, three bureaus.
We hit the mattress with a thud each night, insensible

to the shrieks of pterodactyls, the harsh echo
in the courtyard, great ocean gulls.

But when our truck roars to life outside our window,
like a fox you spring awake in the small

hours, run out the door, swift and naked to foil
the robber, a man whose bulk you grapple

to the ground. As though you had always known
this fight, you rise without clothes and wrestle,

a bear baited by three days of stones.
Your hard body a push, you grab and pull

him from behind the wheel at four a.m., so
when the man escapes down the lane with your smell

still on him, the high twang of adrenalin and low
grunt of fight, you stand in this new city's pall

and wonder why moving house makes us so
fierce and lonely, and just then you fall

prey to the sound of boxcars shunting in the low
distance, our faraway home close as your pants still

slung over the back of a kitchen chair, two floors
up, a thousand miles away from this disquiet, this lull.

Genealogy of Heaven

Here in Heaven, three growing seasons
mean daffodils in February and everyone's
an aesthete, shuddering at the concrete
commerce or flat crops that wasted
their youth. Here in Heaven, rabbits
with fur softer than rainwater
lounge without fear of cats,
who are not allowed in Heaven. (All
felines must be neutered, declawed,
defanged. All canines leashed,
aproned, obedient.) Here
in Heaven, we go for months without
the sun though no one talks about
clouds or how the low squall in
your stomach sours every night. No one talks
about the old man who stands on the edge
of Elysian Fields in nothing but a grimy
vest and sandwich board proclaiming God
a fascist. Everyone wants to live here.
Some say that Heaven herself was better
a hundred years before, when the gingerbread
mansions still stood, furnished with
cedar or jade. People knew about lawn
tennis then, white verbena, the value of
an unobstructed view. Sedate whales swam
in place, baskets spilled
nectar and honey, a proper
cream tea served in the castle on
the parched hill. Those of us not
fit for Heaven spent
our lives back stairs or in
shanty towns, then lay in

graves close enough to the sea to be washed
away in a storm, not in the blood of the lamb,
by the wrath and extreme good
grace of God who proved after all
as we knew he would
to be a fair and good
English
man.

Peaceable Kingdom

The dog down the hall has six black
stitches pulling the skin tight around
his empty sockets like two drawstring purses,
holding pennies for his eyes. He tilts
his head to sniff the bag of potting soil
I carry. The ground has leapt into my arms.
The ferret next door escapes in the night.
We beat the bushes for her, calling
Here, Speedy, here girl though we know
she won't answer. Every broken branch
looks like a ferret stretched thin, making
a break for the road. She is found hungry
the next day, skittering at the fridge door.
My cat curls against the baseboards or thrusts
her voluptuous belly against the wall. She
keeps an eye on birds from behind the curtains,
hangs her tail down, a perfect bellpull.
All our plants are sunburned. Today you want
to know if there were two of you, would I
live with you both? I paint the nails on my
left hand red; the man next door strokes
his moustache and hails you
How are you, you old snake in the grass?
The blind dog nuzzles the ferret, and she spreads
the fine black pads of her paws, reaches up
in surrender, in praise.

Property

I was picking blackberries getting pricked by thorns worth
a little bloodshed when a man appeared in the middle of
the bushes I was having a religious experience no one could
stand in those thorns but Christ with his crown so my
mouth agape my hands red with juice I froze until the
man said

I'd like some of those myself

I thought of all those stories in which God or a trickster
pretends hunger to test the goodness of the mortal I knew it
was right to be generous but then again he was one more
man to feed to gather and cook for so I said

there's enough for everyone   but you'd better get picking

the man's face darkened I could see he was standing on a
path through the bushes he said *this is private property* if my
grandmother was alive she'd be furious at the waste and I
thought of bill bissett and said

hey   nobody owns the earth

I thought that would settle it but the man said

well I own this piece of it get off my land you dirty hippie

I knew he wasn't talking to me someone said those words
to him thirty years ago when he bummed around the island
frazzle-headed finding himself before the family money slept
rough and loved a girl with hair down to her ass he did

all this while I was in kindergarten pining for the
sophistication of grade one where it was rumoured you
could hold the book in your own hands

I offered him the berries I had picked and he said that he
was calling the police to see if I offered them berries when
they slapped me with a trespassing fine so while I waited
for this generous exchange of opposites I climbed back down
to the beach and wondered if the man owned the piece of
ocean in front of his land the water that I went and washed
my dirty hippie feet in while he watched from the bushes
just in case

I stole his share of salt.

La méduse

Day six in exile, you found
a jellyfish on the beach, flipped it over
to show me. The gaping serrated mouth,
the stomach, a green stone
masquerading as its heart. Medusa
with her wave of hair, a nest of sea-snakes,
a sting, a love bite. She tore when you tried
to lift her back to the water, her gelatinous
body rippled and was gone into that great salt flap
we crossed, that stretch of blue that keeps us
begging on this island, fools for this
shallow ground, this short breath.

Arise and Walk

It's a party like any other, loud with gossip
and complaint, when my friend shoulders
through that lattice of bodies gripping glasses
like lifelines, a crowd of bottled shrugs
and canned laughter. My friend crosses
the threshold like a bridegroom, shoulders
like a table. He's been dead for ten years,
now he wears a baseball cap, carries
a frozen pizza. In the kitchen, I watch him
settle the pie onto an oven rack and grin,
still a tease. By what radar has he found me
beside this alien water, far from the palliative
alphabet, that neuropathic pulse of letters?
In ten years, I have grown older, fatter, not
much smarter, but the grave's a quick study;
he has learned Merlin's secret. He lives
backwards, ten years younger and stronger.
He no longer gazes at other men but is married
to a girl with the obsidian eyes of Kali.
His weight is back on his bones, though
he's shed the hunger that clothed us both.
His new family wreathes his neck, smoke
on a scarf. His wife tucks my arm in hers and
tells me about finches, compares wings and beaks,
their perfect fan of feathers. Their small son
screams around the house in a Superman shirt
when leaping from footstools. I corner Lazarus
in the hall, he won't meet my eye. Talks about
the weather, his job tending bar. Finally admits
weariness. *Please,* he says, *I can't tell you.*

Three rooms away, the oven timer rings, the boy
squeals that he hates pepperoni. His father's
green eyes are lit like fireswamps, full of guilt
or judgement, or as at the last days, filled
with what the grave teaches like history teaches, what
it is to know, I can't tell you.

ECCENTRIC ORBIT

Fortes fortuna adiuvat.
Fortune favours the brave.
—Terence, *Phormio*

Blacksmith Quartet

The Village Smithy

Since it's up to me,
I'll start with
the forge, hot
as a catcher's
mitt
after a triple-header,
glowing the same
febrile orange
as a forehead
under the influence,
sweating headwaters, water
of life on the brain.

Up to me to
introduce the grandfather
I never met

Longfellow
stands him
beneath a scrub oak
in his leather apron

(the trouble with family
stories is that
they are never
as good as
they might be if
we didn't know
families, or stories, or
family stories)

if I began with smell,
I would choose
the low hay note
of horse almost
sweet with
grass, but I'm
talking shit
while I've left
my grandfather
beneath the scrub oak
waiting for these
lines while he could be
working, and though
we've never met
I know he'd think
it foolish so

(the trouble with family
stories is the telling
        the making of them
out of air and filings,
stoking the fire
to bend them,
hot iron)

so I'll begin with
horseshoes,
pull my grand-
father away from under
the tree   and put him
by the forge
where he won't
glare at me, a girl

with too much
to say (my mother
said she never
understood a word
he said because
his burr was so
strong, but then she
said he never
said much

to begin with

St. Dunstan

My grandmother allowed
no liquor in her house
because it was the devil's
brew. My mother and father
smuggled a bottle of red wine
up to the top floor room
my grandmother gave them for
their wedding night. My grandmother
kept her powder dry and her house
demon-free. My grandfather's whiskey
stayed in the forge and they
agreed never
to speak of it, agreed the way
two people who do not speak
about the unspeakable
could agree not to
speak.

Halfway through his nightly
dram, my granddad looks up
and the devil's in the doorway,
wanting to wet his whistle,
and granddad thinks, *I'm pickled*
if the old girl wasn't right,
and watches the Lord of Darkness
mooch about for a spot to sit
among the tools and benches.
The forge is no place for a lazy
devil. My granddad snags
Old Nick's nose in a pair of tongs,
yanks it round with a twist of the wrist,
and there's a sick pop as the evil
cartilage crunches in the devil's honker

and he squeals
like a piglet on a rusty hinge.
That's the last straw. My granddad
hates mewlers and drags the devil
to the door by the nose,
boots him in the backside like
you'd boot a hound too stupid
to not eat his own turds.
Off ye go laddie. He nailed a horseshoe
above the doorway, and thought
the worst of it was he couldn't tell
my grandmother, who would be
mad that he was drinking,
but madder still that she had been safe
in her dry house
unable to get her licks in,
my parents perched on high
with their nervous cups of wine.

The Farrier

He walks the line of stables at the fair,
draught horses snort and bump their hocks against

the wooden stalls, toss their manes, turn their
groomed heads to him. No blue ribbons, only

the flesh that pulls the heavy cart, muscle like bound
rope and tackle on the Percherons who

hauled the ancient firewagon with the strength
of their white blazes. The Belgian has four

white gaiters and a tight brisket. One horse stands
eighteen hands at the withers, his head swings out

of the dark like a coal scuttle with eyes. For these
coldbloods, the cavalry farrier turned smithy on

the boat over. The trainers nod and mumble back
to their trailers. The old days. The fairground lurches

like a hurdy-gurdy with daredevil stunts and
salt, with performing dogs who wiggle like piglets

on command, while sows in coloured silks
race around a track. Someone had to shoe

the giant Clydesdale, hold the slim tremble
of fetlock between his thighs and swing a hammer

at that hoof the size of a soup plate. Forge.
Fire. Nail. Hoof. Fair deal. Fair enough.

Inheritance

He passed his lame foot
down to me like potatoes
at Sunday dinner. I took
a helping of that knitted bone
and learned to limp
all on my own. My turned foot
predicts rain and I can make
fire nearly anywhere.

I build a fire at a cabin
one Thanksgiving, and
the neighbour ribs my husband
about how much he likes a girl in
desert boots who can cut
kindling and light a match
on her thigh. *She's a keeper,*
she's not afraid of smoke.

My hands are ash and my
neighbour's wife frowns
at my nails over dinner. She
met her husband when she was
a spinster teacher and the janitor
winked at her every morning
until she married him. The janitor
smiles across the table and
says, *She knew how to bang*
erasers, just before his sleeve
catches fire, too close to the candle
that keeps the gravy warm. Rain
tomorrow. I can feel it.

A Strip of Sky

he was young in the Great War, left Glasgow at eighteen,
bound for Ypres in a wool uniform at the height of June,
served three years in the trenches, climbed the fire steps each
morning and sunset, pinched as many lice and heard as
many larks pierce the dawn as the next man, or at least the
next man who lived

*the crucified Canadian was strung up on a cross of rifles and
left to die, flies laid eggs in his head wound, he knew nothing
but buzzing, saw nothing but a strip of sky despite his strategic
vantage point high above the enemy trench*

wounded at the Somme and gassed at Vimy, he saw the
Angel of Mons rise behind him, her thousand archers poised
with arrows taut on bowstrings and he freed the horses to
shift for themselves in the woods, though some ran towards
the shelling and still he died at Passchendaele, slipped off the
duckboards and drowned in the mud

*he exchanged tinned fruitcake with blond boys in feldgrau,
played a game of soccer to a draw, each man thinking we can
go home now, but the next morning standing at arms, his
stomach twisted from too much schnapps and sweets, he
remembered two dark-haired Germans, the sweeper and the
striker, the ones who said they weren't sad to miss Christmas
because* Wir sind Juden

warned that his children would ask, he told jokes about
French women climbing through windows in torn under-
wear, or no underwear at all, but still climbing through and
over the broken glass, and the awful plonk they all drank
when there was no whiskey, which was all the time and then
he changed the subject

the War to End All Wars outlasted the Armistice, a lie told
back home where everyone was tired of war news, so they
turned into flappers and rum-runners on the new money, while
the war staggered on beneath the weight of the poppies,
troglodyte soldiers gone to ground and the dead unable to stop
mounting the fire step twice a day despite the inconvenience of
rigor mortis

wore his ribbons and crosses on parade every Armistice
Day until 1968, when he buried the medals in their tin box
beneath a dogwood bush, the poisonous berries we were
warned never to touch

Odyssey

1.

My father peels a text
from the top of the pile, a tongue
coming unstuck from a palate.
The teetering tower is chosen for
the fall, its warning weight.
My father opens *The Odyssey*
to page one, and closes it on page
two. I want him to read on and on
until his eyes bleed and his hands
shake. I want him to read of Scylla's
skirt of heads, carping and sniping like
a backseat full of kids in a Ford Galaxy.
I want him to read about the blinded
Cyclops bellowing his fool head
off and the Sirens ululating in vibrato
like Ethel Merman and Kathleen Battle
in some clash of the titan divas.
I want my father to bend
his back and row hard through
Hades, chase the Cattle of the Sun,
that herd of Herefords who won't
come home. But he closes the book
on the wine-dark sea. Tiresias
foretold it. I am not
dead, but a Lotus Eater,
and my father will not eat my
handful of petals, this alarming
bloom of words.

2.

Call it poetic justice
or evolution but
at the bookstore
I am deep into reading
all those straight perfect
spines, when a voice
asks *are you taller
than me?*

I stretch to the top shelf,
thumb down Homer, hand
the man that ruined tower
and he thanks me.

He stands fragrant as mace
but battered, I think, as I drive
my chariot through a wall of fire.
He staggers when I stretch my
mighty wings above him, my hair
singed to the eyebrows, his skirt
tucked between his legs.

Astrophel

1970

Pluto is new, our science teacher said,
found in our own lifetime by men
in white lab coats behind a telescope
more giant than any cartoon. *Gargantuan,*
the boys said, *humungous*, testing words
the size of stellar explosions. They gazed
into a lens as big as a clear manhole cover,
a tunnel to the sky. They tumbled in, amazed
at rogue galaxies, stumbled and fell
in love with the universe, climbed to
the roof of the garage, closer to the spell

of stars. Medieval astronomers stared
from our books with deserted eyes; they saw
the earth move, lost years of their lives
defending their mothers against civil law.
The charge of witchcraft never came clear.
(*An infinity of worlds*, said the women. *Yes,*
said their learned sons, *but not here.*)

1972

Two houses down, a girl plays the cello
all the hot prairie afternoon. Each note
crawls out her window and forms a throbbing sphere
on the front lawn, exactly the size of the globe
of the moon her brother keeps. She'll leave here
to play in an orchestra far away, wear a black
velvet skirt, her long hair twisted back into a spear.
Her brother's allergic to the summer trees; he hacks
his wet cough through seven books about space.
He tells me he can see Mars on a clear night, and
I think we're doomed, the earth a carapace

for our skulls. The ground opens to swallow
me with the first note of Bach. That summer I know
I am mortal. I give him chicken pox
and wear a small crater on my brow,
a moon of Jupiter named for a tenth Muse who
grants small boons to virgins, named Ridiclio.

1978

In junior high, our geography teacher was
a shell-shocked pilot who could navigate
by the stars, those gas giants who hold
planets at arm's length. He'd wait
for us to settle, then stand atop his desk
to teach us the advantage of the aerial view.
He looped string around two thumbtacks
pressed into the chalkboard, swooped and drew
an ellipse, *eccentric orbit,* he said. He'd flown
fifty missions in enemy airspace, beyond any
detection limit. We thought he was an old loon,

sketched him wearing goggles and a leather cap,
made him a wing-walker, a basket case, a sap.
Struck by full-moon engine trouble over unknown
territory. Pilot to bombardier. He checked the map
and bailed out into the stars over Cologne,
his body a bone star in a uniform blown
into the light, parachute taut as skin.
Orion with his sword and lion's pelt, captured alone
waiting out the moon, the first light of dawn.
He saw the winged horse and Bellerophon soar
to race the vulture of Mars, and win. Then he was
home, Icarus in a knitted tie, teaching flight and war:

how an airless planet can support hospitable moons,
how the new planets are not named for gods,
but with strings of numbers, off-world telephones.
An infinity of worlds. Yes. The mothers free to cleave
to pies and bloodwort, the boy raking elm leaves,
the soldier alive to grow old. The titan Hyperion

argued for eccentric orbit as he fathered the sun.

PROVIDENCE

Good fortune deceives, but bad fortune enlightens.
—Boethius, *Consolation of Philosophy,* Book II

Aliena Misericordia

Mercy is foreign. Babies
wrapped tightly to boards
like swaddled worms, thrown
off bridges into canals that wind
through the city, intestinal,
the river a snake that coughs up
children into the arthritic hands of
bishops. Kindness is strange as
spite or the wolf who suckled
twin boys, the brothers who founded
the eternal city before one drew
his sword against the other. The wolf
stood astride the gates, her ribs
a grating. Cowled men and
hooded women passed beneath her
teats and knew themselves
childless as stone, sinful as
brass. Monks and novices
pulled children kicking from
the baptismal current. Pity is
a query, clemency a guess at
motherhood, her awful
red justice. Duty serves the
shriek of a baby who coughs
river water onto a rough robe.

The Kindness of Strangers

(i) *Moses*

He floated mewling downriver to
a womb dry from a royal marriage.
Did she wade into the current, or send
a slave, a woman who might have been
his mother, to test the waters? If
she wanted the boy, the pharaoh's daughter
would have stepped into the river,
a mikvah to cleanse her of her
barren days, a baptism that would ruin
her linen shift, bring her nearer to
the child who would live to see his god burn
and snap in a bush twenty feet away.

Her gods were kind, Isis and Anubis;
she reached for the basket with both hands,
and wept kohl in perfect black stripes
down her cheeks. She and her women
made much of the beloved boy, taught him
to eat locusts, part the sea.

(ii) *Swellfoot*

The goatherd's woman bathed
the baby's feet three times
a day, encased them in a poultice of mint
and kid dung. His fever dropped
but he wouldn't open his eyes. She sucked
splinters from the wounds, squeezed out
thick green pus with her
calloused thumbs. Grateful for
each sliver that poked her tongue, she
spilled the blood of her plumpest
nanny on the red rock, in the dry season.

The boy's shriek at the sound of her steps
meant he was healing, moving by days
away from the bearded man who
swung him by his heels, pegged him
to the olive tree through the pink soles
of his feet, skin that had never touched
ground. Hanging down, his hair
formed a crown.

(iii) *Arthur*

This boy, this sprout, never as tall as
his brother, never as quick to skin
a coney, never hairy, never honed.
A wart on his brother's thumb,
an afterthought or no thought at all.

He sweats daily under his fear of
the falcon's grip in its leather traces.
Beneath its hood, a yellow eye darts,
rolls in defiance of his command,
this brute of feather and sinew,
and he the dragon's son.

Orphines

Anne of Green Gables and Little
Orphan Annie were separated at birth,
born to a mother who may have been
so addled by poverty and labour that
she missed the double blessing, and cursed
them both. Anne, she said. Call her Annie. Perhaps
their fire-engine hair confused her, burned her,
drove her to her death. Perhaps she couldn't
bear the sparrowy yodels spiralling from
their flimsy bassinets, so spunky,
such little fighters. Perhaps she sank
through the tiled floor, linked arms
with her own ghost, leaving Red Baby One
and Red Baby Two until the nuns who ran
the orphanage christened them, named them after
the withered apple tree, last year's tomato vine,
the saint who conceived and bore ripe fruit
after her time. It's true—you can see apples
in the girls' cheeks, tomatoes in their hair.
Not carrots; Anne broke a slate over Gilbert's head,
and right she was. Tomato girls, her and
her sister, and nobody better forget it.
She always said she was dumping this poky
island like a hot potato and lighting out for New
York faster than you could spit. She'd hook
up with her sister, big time, who'd swung
herself one hell of a sweet deal and if only
she could steal something faster
than a leaky rowboat, she'd cut off
her braids with a boning knife and roar
down the coast, eating the spray. She'd
spare no one, not her. She'd
put eyes back in her sister's head;
she'd fill her in on the hard cheese life
in that place where even the soil was red.

Cuckoo

it was simple
i was the biggest
and food was scarce
it only took a minute
to nudge the others over
the edge they fit so snug
on my neck never woke until
they were in flight if she
minded she never said she might
have tipped me out into the air if
she hated me or missed the others
but i gawped open my mouth
and she lowered green
worms into my maw while
their pink bodies blackened
on the ground below us or
were eaten by cats she taught me
to fly i found a cozy nest
one day with a red thread
woven through it a
vein or a prize for
being the smartest

Teacher

She is no witch, that woman with
the handful of blisters, but she can't
close her mouth on the bats
that fly keening from her
throat. She will not suffer fools.
Her fury keeps her warm in the wind.
Her corset an iron maiden. What fat
would dare live on this rack of bone,
this pillory of flesh? She has a long reach.
Don't cross her at cards or over water.
She's not a marshmallow who needs
a soft touch. The first person to slip
sweet poison in her ear will pay.
Women like her are not rubes in love
just because they've had none. Let her be
the first to tell you how famine scrubs
away hunger. Drought dries the land
beyond the simple bliss of a shower. She
reads your sweet talk as a softening of
the brain, the kind she saw every day
in the Bastards Home until her brother
caught a fever in a cardboard coffin. She
stood by his box as the nun with the single
milky eye tangled her in those long black
arms, her mouth scoured with asafoetida.

Old Stories

In the old stories, the baby squalls
in a bundle of rags, handed over like
a sack of kicking potatoes to toothless
peasants, who build a straw pallet
and cover it with sheepskin, maybe wolf-pelt.
The woman weaves coarse brown tunics
for the child, who treks barefoot
through the woods, charming bird and beast,
and grows riotously healthy on a meagre diet
in an unheated cottage, slopping pigs
with a smile, threshing grain by hand.
The young man whistles all the time and
understands how to read the stars. Dumbfounds
the simple couple. One day, they wake
before dawn and tiptoe close to watch him
sleep, blooming with good bones. The faithful
old peasant raises his scythe, still
sharp from the fields. His wife holds
a bowl she carved herself,
to catch the blood.

Home Children Poems

Dr. Barnardo

A boy from the Ragged School
showed the doctor hundreds of boys
asleep in dank Stepney alleys, tired from
fighting dogs for the leavings. Girls
did not sleep but walked all night, eyes shut
against whomever followed, clacking. The red
headed child found curled up in a barrel
like a pickle, dead. The doctor forgot
his trip to China. He shoved
a rich man through the eye of
a needle, wrestled him in the pit of
guilt. He argued out a house,
then a Home, filled them with boys who
didn't understand a clean shirt, or a man's
orders. No destitute child refused
admission. Porridge
every morning. Bread and
treacle every night. Forty pairs
of shoes to clean of mud and dung,
polish before sleep. A Bible for each
boy, and the doctor's photo. Many lost
the Bibles in moves between farms in
the land they thought was a story
until they disembarked, or later in the army
where they fought as poor boys
have fought and died forever,
the photo of a man they thought was
god their father lost with
the Good Word.

Five Shillings

At the first Home, Dr. Barnardo
filled a room with phials of silver
iodine and collodion, a box with
stork's legs covered by a black
curtain. He took an admission
photo of each child, and another
three months later, when Home life had
puffed their cheeks, thickened
their arms, explained the idea of
a smile. He sold the photos, before
and after shuffled together like
a pair of aces in a short deck. He
asked for five shillings and raised
eyebrows. What gentleman could
flip through these photos and not
give twice, three times
the price?

Barnardo knew how to give people
the business. He doctored the photos, tore
the boys' clothes so that men would throw
pound notes across the pond even
after the sweetest boys shipped over
to Canada. He fathered six children, including
a girl whose torn chromosome kept her young
forever. He acted as sovereign lord and
philanthropic abductor to thirty thousand
children. In his studio shot, the doctor's

eyes are recessed and hot, his mutton chops
straggly, his skin dewy as a girl's. What will
you give me for this photo of the good
doctor, pick of the litter, best of breed,
flower of the flock? Five shillings?
Two?

Flower of the Flock

I was told there was a farmer who
wanted a boy like me.

I thought Canadians had no
children, cursed by God or
the climate, or their sons foolish,
daughters dull enough to be deaf to
a buffalo stampede and trampled.
Canada was a place where only
the fleet of foot could dart
out of range.   I saw
a daguerreotype of men on horseback,
lording it over the beasts, so I shook
the agent's hand and climbed
the gangplank, crawled down
into the foul hold and thought
a smart lad like me
ought to get his hands
on one of those horses.

The boat trip over was not
too exciting, except that I fell
in love for the first time. A girl
held my seasick head in her lap, and I could
never thank her for it, for I could not
find where she was sent, though I wrote
the Home and begged.

We saw pails hanging from
trees and wondered why. We
scrubbed the floor at the Home
three times a week, but there was
nothing to scrub in the forest,
though the trees bled.   A white stripe
moved like a whip in the sheep pen
and I screamed there was a snake,
until the farmer shot the skunk and
hauled it out by the tail to show me,
its tiny cat face so small that
the next night, I tossed rocks
at a shapeless animal ahead on the road,
then walked by where it sat in the dark,
its breath huffing like a bellows.
The farmer showed me claw marks high
on the sticky trunk of a maple so
I would understand how big a bear was.

Good Conduct

But whoso shall offend
                    (whip, starve, freeze)
one of these little ones which believe in me,
                         (Dr. Barnardo, Maria Rye, God)

it were better for him that a millstone
                    (a slop pail, a turkey carcass, a plough) be
hanged around his neck and that he
were drowned in the depth of the sea
                    (buried in silage, worked to dropping). Woe

unto the world because of offences!
                    (theft, a fist, a pitchfork) For it must
needs be that offences come   (influenza, flood, hail);

but woe to that man
                    (or woman, those starved and starving
homesteaders) by whom the offence cometh!
                         (rape, neglect, bloodflowers)

Bliss

Every Home girl wanted her own
floors to sweep, beans to can,
children to feed and wipe and comb
clean. A Home girl's strong backbone
twisted her, aged her into a sweet crone
who baked endless lemon pies,
who whipped meringue into cones,
enough to please but not to awe. Home
boys wore wedding rings like coins
on their grindstone hands, a balm
against those nights when they woke
from a nightmare of nothing to own,
forty below and the ground like bone,
flax like a rumour of smoke.

                Other boys groaned
into bachelors who walked
thirty miles a day, railway drones
or on the bum. A lone
Home girl rode the rails, delivered
herself from a tramp who
came at her with a heavy stone,
took him down with
a boning knife to his liver,
then shrugged into his pants, owned
his coat. Boiled her billy on a flame
beside his pale body without a quiver.
The farmer interfered with her for seven
years, every time his wife took
the gig into town to sell eggs, never
saw the girl grow thin as a blade.
One thrust made her into the man.
She banked her campfire, shivered.

VIRTUE OF NECESSITY

Then hate me when thou wilt, if ever, now,
Now while the world is bent my deeds to crosse,
Joyne with the sight of fortune, make me bow.
    —Shakespeare, *Sonnet XC*

Foster

I am the bird that nested in
the family tree after
thirteen days over desert. A yellow
branch wove twigs into a bowl.
The wind piped a hatching
song through its knitted lips.
I whistled the only tune
I knew, and preened.

I am the stray dog that sniffed
the family tree for
the scent of others. I stayed
for the boy who fed me at sundown,
for the girl who combed ticks
from my fur with her fingers
and pinched them dead.

I am the tramp who slept beneath
the family tree when
leaves dropped on my thin
coat and covered me. I curled
into the hollow trunk, a root
pillow. I own nothing,
but when I go, I will leave
a ring with a green stone
that will fit no finger.

Brilliant Disguise

She quit smoking the day she met
her mother. Everything tasted charred;
the sweet potato pie and cappuccino,
pumice. A film of ash floated
in her water glass. *I own my own
business*, said her mother on the phone, so
she looked for an older woman in a smart
blue suit, a woman with no one but herself
to pamper, a woman used to long hours,
hard work, earned luxury. She looked for
herself. But the woman wore a cardigan and
flowered blouse, like someone's mother
rigged out for Hallowe'en as herself.
The woman didn't even have the red hair
her father remembered. She paid the bill,
went home, and threw away her lighter,
her cigarettes, three boxes of Miss Clairol #34:
Autumn Sienna.

The Family Way

(i) *Mother*

We wanted. We waited.
We would have taken
any one offered,
blind or deaf or ill,
a baby to fill the house,
the hollow place scraped
inside us, the hole
we had not dug. We checked
the church doorstep every night
for baskets. Two doors down,
our neighbour's boy was born
with fleshy hooks for hands,
three fingers knit together
by a thick skin. His mother
wouldn't look at him, his eyes
blue sparks above his waving
claws. We would have taken him
and been glad for two fingers,
for a piece of bone and gristle
not quite a thumb.

When we got the call, that night
in January, I stripped off
my wet apron, and called
down to the basement, where
my husband was planing
a door level. He took
the stairs three at a time,
had the car backed out
before I could run
a comb through my hair.
We crossed the bridge

and on the frozen river,
I saw an open patch of water,
a shiny gash in the ice,
dark as the blood
that came every month.
I said *I'll be a mother*
in half an hour, and
he tightened his grip
on the steering wheel,
guiding the car over
the icy roads, as though
the baby, our baby, as though
you were already
asleep in the back.

(ii) *Mother II*

I left town for a year. My parents
told everyone I went away to
a special school in the city
to learn French. When I came back, I never
went to dances or anywhere else alone.
The town always let me know
I didn't get away with it, showed
no one was fooled by my
disappearing act, the way I conjured
a narrow future. I could not pull
the wool over the town's all-seeing eye
with some big-city magic, a virgin birth,
or a belly with no baby. I waited for
someone to *parlay-voo* me,
at choir practice or a bake sale,
even though they spoke no more French
than I did, but still I set great store
by waiting, as though it would prove
something, this test,
my silence.

Proof

Down the lane, the girl-goof brays,
a hound on the scent and I'm crazed
as a fox. Her mouth howls wide enough
to swallow me and my impossible truth.
She tails me and yowls for incontrovertible proof
that he's my brother, because one roof

shelters us. I offer her my back. Her arms flail,
rough justice leaves me bruised, aloof

to those big-mouthed girls who poke
at any sore to see it bleed, who revoke
my right to this birth, this solid food,
this house by the lane, my good
pitching arm. I will not brood
over the noise of need or opaque smoke.

Unheimlich

At school, we don't fool ourselves;
we are Jews and Christians, we know
who we are. During the Yom Kippur War,
the Jewish boys paste a sticker of the flag
of Israel on the arms of their jackets,
blue and white. They bump up against
anyone who stares in the hall,
on the playground. It's October, it's war,
the boy with all the answers is the class hero.
He struts the hopscotch tarmac, wearing
his Star of David in the very centre
of his back, a target. Herschel and Larry
Lutz wear stars too, even Herschel with
his brain-boy's glasses and little-old-man
walk, even Larry tall, blond. Larry's a goy
in the house of love, he's Zeppo Marx,
Paul Newman in *Exodus*, Olivier's Shylock.
When the Lutzes adopted Larry, he was
a scrawny boy who wept whenever Herschel
was carried from the room. October ends,
and the boys peel the flags from their jackets.
Larry wears his star to a grey paste
on his left arm, walks home with Herschel
every day. One of these things is not like
the other. At eleven, I am taller than
my father, a pale gift of height. Larry and I
grow into strangers in our fathers' houses,
unheimlich, mischling, not quite
old enough to worry about skin, hair,
an extra four inches of leg. We are in
grade six; we know ourselves.

Rotten

One girl made us all look
bad; the year we were thirteen,
she wore tight sweaters
and blabbed to anyone about
being adopted, wasn't above
leveraging sympathy out of
the strict Baptist eye of the
handsomest boy in school,
the boy we called Brother
Bruce. Straight and saved,
his white shirt rode on his
shoulders like wings and
aged him almost into an adult,
someone closer to Heaven
than the rest of us scrubbers.
He was not a fool who would
fall for one girl's pout,
her deep love of shock. But
it only took a week for Brother
Bruce to trip. He stumbled in the hall
between classes, a broken seraph.
His glasses never sat straight
on his nose again. His spine slid
like a trombone, but the girl
was done. She lay on her back
across the ping-pong table,
languid as a lizard, while I
tied the net tight. She peeled
the rubber off her paddle in
a long loose strip, and said,
Brother Bruce was all right,
but I'm ready for a man. I served
the little white ball before she could
sit up. It hit her hard in the breast and

I was glad the ball went where I
could not, straight to her inveterate
badness, her rotten core. I wanted to
reach my hand into her fetid heart
and yank the tumour out of her,
slug the invertebrate mass of her
guts, pummel her to sense. I
wanted to say, *stop slutting*
around or you'll get us all
in trouble, sent back, locked up,
burned at the stake. She batted the ball
back at me, casual as a sailor, wanting
to win but not wanting to want,
a strip of rubber flapping
on her paddle, a loose-lipped mouth.

The Father

He must have grown
a paunch by now, good
on a man that tall. The extra
weight balances him like
a bowling pin, those pounds
he tried to gain when it mattered,
when he was fifteen and his
spaghetti arms taunted him in
the bathroom mirror, nineteen and
the smallest man working in
the lumberyard, twenty in the autumn,
back in school to make himself
a man, build bridges, reservoirs.

The girl from the lake gained weight
that looked like a shotgun levelled
at his flat stomach. He signed
the form, never saw the child, grew
a little taller. He blueprinted

skyscrapers for decades, and grunts
when he sits or unwinds from
a chair—old man noise. His daughter
meets him at the door, relieves him of
briefcase and coat. She mixes his martini
and hears his weight creak into the leather

recliner. She doesn't know he made
his first free-standing structure without
a plan. A prototype, a stab in the dark, product
to be refined later—crude oil, or nickel before
the slag's poured off his youth
made large; what
a skinny boy will do
to make himself
bigger.

Parenting Lessons

On my way to the house of a friend who never wanted
children but adopted her partner's boys who made her a
grandmother, she who whips out photos even as she swears
she never changed a diaper. On the splintered benches of
the ferry, the island gossip is a fence with broken pickets.
One man talks about the daughter who tracked him down
after twenty years, and laughs at the girl's dumb luck and
perseverance, his sudden slipshod fatherhood. He says, *why
bother raising children? Just wait until they're reasonable adults
then let them find you—if they can.* He laughs like a drain.

A woman tells him that her son has never held a job and
lives on the street, but is six foot four with lots of friends,
and he's in an upgrading program, which ought to change
everything. She tells him that she's in the garbage business
on the island, took it over from a woman who left for
Guatemala for three years, but came back after three months,
wanted her cottage and business back. But *a deal's a deal,*
says the woman on the ferry. So the woman who didn't like
Guatemala is unemployed and has to live with her daughter,
who's trying to raise these two kids she's got all on her own.
*Yep, that house is pretty cramped with the four of them, tough
break all around.*

The unexpected grandmother breaknecks her Jeep down the
island road. She takes a corner on two wheels and says *you
don't have to explain yourself to me.*

Museum

My face a wide-angle lens, a museum piece beside the totem
pole, I pose with a big-mouthed frog, a bottom feeder. He's
the trickster, I'm the trick. The frog's toothless lips next to
my face wide as a plate and white as dough, mask of the egg
donor, first and other mother, wolf in girl's clothing. That
sixth sense, that fifth wheel. Ghost. She doesn't know three's
a crowd. Her face, mine, the face of a woman with a recipe
box full of meat and noodle casseroles. My hair grows long
against my will, braids itself in loops and wraps around my
head. A dirndl skirt latches onto me, asks to be smoothed
over my hips. With a spade as broad as my back, in my apron
with eyelet trim, I am digging up the alluvial soil. I uncover
the pelvic bones of my mother, I yawn open my pink gums
and say, *you can see that she had a child early.* I smile at the
archaeology students, who are bored and sweaty with the toil
of digging up my mother. They think they'd like theirs to
stay buried. I smile at their perfect young scowls as I turn
from tadpole into frog, from a wiry smoking whipcord into a
matron making bean soup that could feed the whole crew of
diggers, a woman in flour up to her elbows, a woman who
cuts bread in slices as wide and white as her face.

Human Genome Project

This morning, the argument in class is about purity.
Disputes about hybridity. The talk is about race, about
métissage. We clear our throats and speak. In fractions and
percentages. Numbered days. Half-white, we say, half-native,
one-sixth, 10%. Some cite the one-drop rule. We say
full-blood, half-breed, status, tradition, land claims, and the
Ojibwa student with red hair watches us out of her blue eyes.
We talk race as though it's clear broth, when it's a gumbo, a
stew made without recipe. An African folk tale tells of white
beings escaping the Maker's sack, half-baked, raw, not ready
yet to be people. We the savage. We the barbarous. We the
people. The professor reminds us that we share 90% of our
DNA with chimpanzees.

We want to argue the sex lives of our grandparents without
saying sex and grandparents in the same sentence. No one
says a thing about country marriages and adulteries and
lusts, barren wives and fecund spinsters, babies who were left
behind or traded like sacks of flour. We ignore rape and
orphans and adoption, children who looked like no one and
grew tall anyway. No one knows better; bastards live long and
healthy lives. Husbands trapped the bush for months at a
time, and there was always this year's baby. We can't explain
our faces or our names.

The woman who calls herself after the plants that grow
outside her door is exactly who she says she is.

Doppelgänger

We sit over seafood after skating
the frozen river. These lobster
never waved their pincers beneath pack ice,
we never skimmed over their heads,
but we crunch down on them as though
we are gods, as though we have mastered
something greater than water.
The couple at the next table
complain. The wine. The menu. The weather.
The man chops the blunt air, asks
how fresh are the berries? The waitress nods,
mild, polite. I whisper to you what I
want her to say. *It's winter, you asshole.*
Bite me. No dessert for you. He's
eaten a lot of spit in his day.

The waitress is my double, all
tall women begin as my twin sisters
and drift into my shoulder, my thigh.
She brings coffee and brandy
snifters big as bowls for both of us.
I am her, she is me, we walk back
to the kitchen in our shared body.
You follow, telling the joke
you always tell when I, when you are tipsy.

The brandy collects you a scowl
and a sniff from the spit-eater's wife,
the sheen of venom on her lips reflects
the candle flame, the snow, your brown eyes,
my teeth when I laugh, the swirl of the cream
you pour into your coffee but do not stir.

Prayer

Bless mother and father and fate and circumstance and reincarnation and karma. Bless God and social services and the women who said it's the best you can give her. Bless the egg and the sperm and the band that played the song they danced to. Bless she who gave and he who gave when they sat down to sign the form. Bless the nurses at the birth who wrapped me up and packed me down the hall. Bless the doctor who said it was right with the voice of a lord and she who dared not argue. Bless the sedative. Bless the grandmother and the congregation and everyone who must have nodded and said yes a baby is a blessing. Bless the worker who made the home visits and wrote the child seems to display the proper attachment. Bless the signed documents, the sealed file, the blue certificate, bless the accident of birth.

As accidents go, it was small, like most slips of the tongue, like a short silence, like the day your father came home tired and your mother baked flour biscuits and they tumbled into bed before they knew what they were about.

There you were. Bless you.

Farewell Symphony

The concertmaster is pregnant, round
as a kettledrum in her velvet dress.
Her violin, a snug and polished cat
beneath her chin. Her bow, a quivering
swallow, swoops the first
note to slacken our limbs,
loosen our spines, melt the metal rod
of our vertebrae. All of us in good
wool and worsted slump in our seats.

Her swaying arm pulls a cry
from wood and horsehair, it
sings a hot poultice onto our aching
hands, swollen faces, bruised eyes.
The dark planet of her body spins
us to sleep. She tiptoes to
the wings, careful not to wake
us, her violin held out in both
hands, a divining rod, offering,
her first born, the moon
descending into a pond.

Notes

15th-century scholar Joseph Moxon wrote several books that explore methods of celestial navigation, including his 1679 volume *Mathematicks Made Easier, or a Mathematical Dictionary explaining the terms of difficult phrases used in arithmetick, geometry, astronomy, astrology and other mathematical sciences.*

Carolyn Abraham's *Possessing Genius: The Bizarre Odyssey of Einstein's Brain* (Viking, 2001) recounts the full story of Dr. Thomas Harvey and the celebrated cerebellum.

Film of Thomas Edison's electrocution of an elephant may be seen in Errol Morris' documentary *Mr. Death: The Rise and Fall of Fred A. Leuchter, Jr.* (2000).

Prof. Robert Smith first mentioned Auden's nocturnal eccentricities to me, following Humphrey Carpenter's *W.H. Auden: A Biography* (Houghton Mifflin, 1981).

The story of Tamar is discussed in *The Book of J*, by Harold Bloom and David Rosenberg (Random House, 1990). I thank Keith Louise Fulton for bringing this text to my attention.

Hugh MacLennan's essay "Boy Meets Girl in Winnipeg and Who Cares?" appears in *Scotchman's Return* (Macmillan, 1960).

The reference to bill bissett in "Property" is to *nobody owns th earth* (House of Anansi Press, 1971).

The legend of the crucified Canadian and other WWI apocrypha from "A Strip of Sky" can be found in Paul Fussell's *The Great War and Modern Memory* (Oxford UP, 1975).

"Aliena Misericordia" and "The Kindness of Strangers" take their titles from James Boswell's *The Kindness of Strangers: The Abandonment of Children in Western Europe from Late Antiquity to the Renaissance* (Pantheon, 1988).

The first line of each stanza of "Flower of the Flock" is taken from a letter written by child emigrants to Canada, published in Phyllis Harrison's *The Home Children* (Watson and Dwyer, 1979). Used with permission.

Dr. Barnardo's Good Conduct medal, engraved with the text of Matthew 18: 5, was bestowed on Home children who displayed exemplary politeness and industry in the homes to which they had been "boarded out."

Acknowledgements

Thanks to the Manitoba Arts Council, for awarding me a Writer's "B" Grant and giving me the time to write much of this book.

Thanks to everyone at Turnstone Press for their hard work and commitment to poetry. Special thanks to Dennis Cooley, veteran of vivisecting verbiage.

Thanks to the editors of the publications in which these poems originally appeared: *Arc, Contemporary Verse 2, Event, Fiddlehead, Grain, Henry Street, Other Voices, Prairie Fire,* and *PRISM International,* in the anthologies *Mocambo Nights* (Ekstasis, 2001), *The Mentor's Canon* (Broken Jaw Press, 2001) and *The Madwoman in the Academy* (University of Calgary Press, 2003), and in my chapbook, *Sass* (Transparent Press, 2001).

I acknowledge the hard work of the organizers and the ears of the audiences of the Mocambo Café Reading Series in Victoria, the Café Libra Reading Series in Vancouver, the Art Bar in Toronto, and Speaking Crow in Winnipeg for their responses and support.

Thank you to the Seattle Art Museum, for displaying Gustav Courbet's *Toilette of the Dead Woman* in August 2002, and to Sharanpal for looking with me.

Thanks to my parents.

"Requiem" is for Jeanette Lynes.

"The Father" is for Miranda Pearson, because she wondered.

"Arise and Walk" won the Bliss Carman Award for Poetry in 2003, and is dedicated to the memory of Ted Karavidas.

"Jezebel" won the "Beyond Feminism" Millennial Poem Contest sponsored by *Other Voices* in 2000.